FUNNY
DICTIONARY

Fabulous Words,
Frazes and Silliquisms

D1737134

MARK FRIEDMAN

markatfpsi@gmail.com

parsepublishing@gmail.com

To order additional copies go to
amazon.com

ISBN: 9798756693904
Imprint: Independently published

Edition 1.1
November 2021

Cover design and interior composition by Ross Feldner, New Age Graphics
newagegraphicsonline.com

FUNNY DICTIONARY
Fabulous Words, Frases and Silliquisms

Contents

This page intentionally left blank

to make the book seem longer.

PROLOGUE

Most of what comes after the Introduction in this book is intended to be read out loud. And even better, you can make it into a game where each person must use the word(s) in a sentence. If the people in your group have no sense of humor, then carefully take this book and put it in a safe place, and wait for the right people to show up.

Funny Dictionary Quality Control Report (excerpt):

Some of this stuff is not funny at all. We recommend reducing the advertised humor quotient, and changing the title to Somewhat Funny Dictionary.

INTRODUCTION

(Skip this if you want.)

I wanted the title of this book to be "Alice's Dictionary" in honor of Lewis Carroll, but worried that it would be seen as **arrogantial**. And, because this work is different from his, it could serve to misrepresent him. But it must be said from the start that he is one of the all time greatest **inspirationers** and **permissioners** when it comes to word play.

Lewis Carroll gave us many things but the most important may be the idea that words can be fun. He showed us exactly how. And then, in an act of **enclapable** generosity, gave us permission to go forth and play. Of course words were always fun and we used this permission long before Lewis Carroll came along. But we didn't always know

---

What's UP

It's easy to understand UP, meaning toward the sky or at the top of the list, but when we awaken in the morning, why do we wake UP ?

At a meeting, why does a topic come UP ? Why do we speak UP, and why are the officers UP for election and why is it UP to the secretary to write UP a report? We call UP our friends, brighten UP a room, polish UP the silver, warm UP the leftovers and clean UP the kitchen. We lock UP the house and fix UP the old car.

At other times, this little word has real special meaning. People stir UP trouble, line UP for tickets, work UP an appetite, and think UP excuses.

To be dressed is one thing but to be dressed UP is special.

And this UP is confusing: A drain must be opened UP because it is stopped UP.

We open UP a store in the morning but we close it UP at night. We seem to be pretty mixed UP about UP !

To be knowledgeable about the proper uses of UP , look UP the word UP in the dictionary. In a desk-sized dictionary, it takes UP almost 1/4 of the page and can add UP to about thirty definitions.

If you are UP to it, you might try building UP a list of the many ways UP is used. It will take UP a lot of your time, but if you don't give UP, you may wind UP with a hundred or more.

When it threatens to rain, we say it is clouding UP. When the sun comes out, we say it is clearing UP. When it rains, it soaks UP the earth. When it does not rain for awhile, things dry UP. One could go on and on, but I'll wrap it UP, for now, my time is UP !

Source: anonymous email

---

we had it. He nailed it to the church doors. He ran it as a banner headline in all the newspapers. He tapped a deep well that has gushed forth ever since.

It is not an automatic notion that words can be fun. Think of the words used in an operating room. It is not good medical etiquette to point out that the word "scalpel" is derived from an act of barbarity. When flying an airplane, jokes about "altitude," and "descend" are rightly frowned upon.

Why are words fun? **First, words take things from two infinite sets and smack them together: Sound and Meaning.** Some of these infinity on infinity combinations are fun to say (e.g. "Hickenlooper")[1]. These are actually the first two of four infinities involving words. We shall get to the other two shortly.

Because of this compounding of infinities, the actual number of recognized words in English and all the other languages combined is just a fraction of all possibilities. This means that there is no such thing as a finished dictionary. The unabridged *Oxford English Dictionary* has almost 500,000 entries. But this is a paltry sum compared to the billions of possible sound-meaning combinations. And there are new ones every day entering the formal and informal lexicons of the world. I hope this book makes a small contribution. What is also interesting about the OED is that it represents a remarkable historical compendium of stand-alone ideas that have, at various points in time, become valuable enough to warrant separate verbal signals. Of course, no actual English speakers need that many words. The average active vocabulary for an adult English speaker is only about 20,000 words. But there's no limit on the number of ideas that can be conveyed with those "few" words.

Many word sounds have more than one meaning, which is not actually surprising given the limited number of phonemes in any given language. One of the most prolific is the word "up." See the box on the previous page with 40 different usages (and another 180 in Part II below). Another **unique combinationism** is the word "fast" which has four meanings in **two pairs of opposites.**

>   1a. Fast as in "to move quickly."
>   1b. Fast as in "to hold fast" and therefore not move at all.

HUMAN INFINITIES

Numbers that seem infinite to most humans but are not. A range of numbers that lie beyond the largest number that normal, regular (non-mathematical) humans can (comfortably) conceive. The number of grains of sand on all the world's beaches or number of stars in the sky are commonly used examples. The term "infinity," as used in this section refers mostly to "human infinities."

The size of human infinity will vary by person and circumstance. Scientists and mathematicians are trained to think about actual infinities, so they don't count except when it comes to the complex compounding of infinities. Even a simple fractal has an infinity of infinities.

---

[1] My apologies to the Hickenlooper family. You must be used to this by now.

2a. Fast as in "to abstain from eating," often as a religious duty.

2b. Fast as a descriptor of purportedly "immoral behavior."

English has so many great standard beginnings and endings that can be used to create new words. And these words are fun because they are fun to say and funny at the same time. **canaryism**: The belief that canaries will one day rule the world. **prefix**: to fix something before it is broken.

The fun of reading words out loud is even better when the words are pure nonsense. From fairy tales and movies we have **Rumpelstiltskin**. And then, of course, there is the most famous of them all: **Supercalifragilisticexpialidocious**.

Nonsense words often have an emotionally implicit meaning that we sense without fully ascribing a definition. Supercalifragilisticexpialidocious obviously describes something that is super or exceptional. Fragilistic conveys both "delicate" and possibly "futuristic." And of course "expiala" implies something happening quickly. "Docious" is the ending that makes it all into an adjective that can be applied to any proper or improper noun. So the feel of this word is of something wonderfully delicate and coming fast. We'll leave Rumpelstiltskin alone for now.

Some new words have parts that don't seem to belong together: **challahpenòs**: spicy braided bread. And some new words can be created by putting together two widely disparate ideas: **boom-meringues: pastries that fly off and return, smacking you in the face.**

My sister Janet, and brother Ken and I are **Scrabble** "enthusiasts," well trained by our dearly departed mother Serene. We love playing Scrabble and will play any time we are together. Many Scrabble-playing families have adopted rules that are not in the official rule book. Our family rules include recirculation of blanks and drawing an extra tile and putting one back at each turn. One of my favorite forms of Scrabble is **Nonsense Scrabble**. In this game, you can put any word on the board as long as you can define it. Instead of keeping score, you keep a list of words and definitions. My favorite is one that my Mom invented years ago, **troupela**: a small troop of Jewish Boy Scouts. You can start to see where this dictionary comes from.

Now if words themselves can have an infinite number of sound-meaning combinations, then sentences add a **third infinity**. **Steven Pinker** cites the case of the world's longest sentence, 500 words in all. He adds "He said she said" to the beginning, which sets in motion a theoretical expansion to infinity. So word play doesn't stop with the words themselves but with the way those words can be used in larger constructions. Homage must be paid again to Lewis Carroll for the best of nonsense speech and nonsense poetry (**jabberwocky**). See the amazing possibilities in the many pure nonsense examples in the dictionary below. Even here there is meaning that is given by context. And that is the **fourth infinity**.

So to recap: The **conphonabulous constructionism** for any word is created by compounding the following four infinities:

+ Sounds (any combination, any length)
+ Meaning (including intended, implied, supplementary and subordinate)
+ Placement in sentence construction, and
+ Placement in the world (experiential, environmental and imaginary contexts).

RIM SHOTS

What do you call a tree that's unfaithful?
Treesonous.

What do you call hair that has been severely rebuked?
Upbraided.

Why is it dangerous to have a frog in your throat?
You might croak.

What do you call an unpleasant pig?
Boorish.

What about a pig with possibilities?
Pygmalion.

How do you get from one foot to the other.
A footbridge.

What's another word for stupid?
What's your name?

What do you call a horse with a raspy throat?
Hoarse.

What is the form of government where Hippos are in charge?
Hippocracy.

A word about how many words are enough for a book like this. If this were "just" the construction of an English dictionary, then the choices would be somewhat easier and one could decide on a cutoff short of the OED (Check out the highly recommended book *Word by Word* by **Kory Stamper**). With made-up words it can never be clear how many words you need before it's enough. This book has grown over many years (decades actually) and now contains more than 1,000 entries. In a recent ruling, the **International Dictionary Advisory Board** (IDAB) has decided that is enough. "Entry," in this case, means any word that is defined or otherwise used for humorous purposes. This includes over 700 actual definitions and more than 300 words used in other constructions.

The dictionary that follows brings some new words into existence and allows some old words to take on new meaning. You must provide your own sentences and context. All this to say that this book just scratches the surface of what is possible.

Some notes on techniques for constructing funny words

1. The first and purest technique is to find an existing word and give it a new meaning: For example **calabash**: to say mean things about California.

2. Find a word and change its meaning by adding or subtracting letters. For example: **acrobait**: substance used to lure reluctant circus performers into death-defying leaps.

3. Add prefixes such as: de- dis- inter- mis- neo- non- pre- post- re- under- over- up- semi- sub- super- and many more.

4. And endings: -ate -ation, -ism, -ocious, -ometer, -oscopy, -saurus and many more.

5. Smash any two words together. This can take the form of a game I created years ago where several pages were filled with one syllable words or word fragments and paired at random (e.g. beefat and clownbin). The creative thinking came with groups of two or more discussing the possible definitions and uses.

And, finally, there should be rules about **tastefulness**, given the **tastelessness**, including overt **racism** and **sexism**, found in some other efforts like Ambrose Bierce's *Devil's Dictionary* (1906). **No jokes about race, gender, ethnicity, sexuality or sexual orientation.** A few jokes about politics and religion are OK because religion and politics take themselves much too seriously. (Jokes in this book about politics are **left-leaning**. Jokes about religion are **irreverent**. In total less than about 20. Proceed at your own risk.) The general rule is to make it funny **for** people not **about** people. (Apologies again to the Hickenlooper family.)

A few more gnotes:

Part II below provides interesting word pairs (and longer lists) that dramatically flip meanings, often with the change of a single letter: **meditation..... medication.** And Part III lists words that are just funny sounding in and of themselves (e.g. **collywobble**). These are the most fun to say and can be spoken in the form of a nonsense poem.

Questions about Certain Words

π Why do caregiver and caretaker mean the same thing?

π Why do "fat chance" and "slim chance" mean the same thing?

π Why do "slow down" and slow up" mean the same thing?

π Why is it called "after dark" when it is really "after light?"

π Why is the third hand on a watch called the second hand?

(Why π? Because it's irrational.)

For a number of years, the *Washington Post* famously sponsored a contest for funny words, much along the lines of what this book purports to do. The winners are some of the best funny words of all time. Since they have circulated for many years on the internet, I believe it is OK to include them here with attribution. There are 30 of these words placed in one of three lists at the end of the book.

Please take this effort as a starting point and make up your own words and definitions. Send them to me and I will include them with attribution in future editions, subject, of course, to International Dictionary Advisory Board review.

How to use this book (mechanically and technically)

Paper version: Find a comfortable place to sit. Place the book on your lap, front cover side up. Use your left hand to grasp the edge of the cover and turn it to the left. Continue doing this until you find something you want to read. (If you have problems using an actual paper book, seek the advice of an older person.)

Electronic version: Open the file. Scroll, Swipe, Click, Clack, Left, Right, Up, Down until you find something you want to read. (If you have problems with this, seek the advice of a younger person.)

How to use this book for just plain fun

It is just fun to read the entries out loud. At a party each person picks a word at random and explains it to the group; or uses it in a sentence or maybe even a full-on writing exercise[2]. All of this might be helped by some form of safe **innebrialism**.

You should know that, in putting this book together, I rejected many dozens of words that didn't make the grade. (Imagine how bad **they** were.) So some definitions are better than others. Just go with the ones that work for you.

As a final gnote, I am an **invertebrate** punster.

Thanks for joining me on this crazy journey.

All Best Wishes

Mark Friedman
Santa Fe, November 2021

---

2 My wonderful wife, Terry Wilson, is a creative writing teacher at the Santa Fe Community College and is always trying to get people to write. She is the author of the hilarious book: *Confessions of a Failed Saint*.

PART I

Funny Words

(finally)

abolonyism: the belief that shellfish will one day rule the world.

absentreeism: deforestation. "Why are these absentrees not showing up for class?"

absolution: restorative skin cream for the abdomen. You can be forgiven if you decide not to use it that way.

abstain: to keep from spilling wine on the rug.

abysmalt: The worst milkshake (or scotch) you'll ever have.

accidental: inadvertent tooth loss.

accommodating: doing whatever your date wants to do.

accordion: the musical instrument used during peace negotiations and marriage counseling.

accumulatte: steady increase in the consumption of fancy coffee drinks.

acidophallus: reproductive organ of male acidophili.

acrobait: substance used to lure reluctant circus performers into death-defying leaps.

Administer: British civil servant responsible for advertising.

adoor: to deeply admire passageways.

adurable: long lasting cuteness.

alarmism: The belief that being in a constant state of fear will make you more vigilant and therefore safe. See also worryism. See also republicons.

alarmism

alimentary school: place where you learn to eat and get fat.

alimoany: state of complaining about spousal payments.

aloof: attitude of superior loofs looking down on other loofs.

amphibianism: a form of species inbetweenism. (see inbetweenism)

anacondo: ownership property for snakes.

anecdotalize: to turn real experience into an anecdote. (Tom D.)

Apostrophy: annual punctuation award.

appoximation: estimated chance that you will get sick.

arcane: out-of-date walking stick.

archery: the design and construction of arches.

arch-enemy: form of delusion where architectural constructs are seen as threatening. "I wouldn't walk under that if I were you."

Archetype: divinely endorsed font. **Helvetica** or **Times Old Roman**. Or more likely, *Gothic.*

Aria 51: alien opera.

asalt: the aggressive use of salt.
  "My dinner was heavily asalted."

aspire: the desire to ascend church steeples.

assinine: part of a scale from zero to total
  assininity. Nine is pretty bad.

atheism: a non-prophet organization.

Aria 51

Atonies: Annual Yom Kippur award for the greatest
  forgiven sin.

atoon: regret expressed by cartoon character.

autodidact: person who won't stop talking about cars.

autograph: visual display of car sales.

auto-mated: internet marriage. "We were automated."

bamboozle: to confuse people by getting them drunk.

bandaid: special charity event for needy bands.

bandwidth: average (sometimes cumulative total) waist size of band members.

bar-ometer: instrument that measures the number of bars in a given area; also device showing how much time is left until "last drink."

batter: a versatile substance that can be used to bake cakes and play baseball.

battering ram: male sheep suckered into knocking down walls.

beecalmed: sedated bee.

beecoming: gathering of bees.

beehooves: the sound of approaching bees.

behemoth: very large moth.

beon: elementary particle responsible for existence.

Bermuda Shorts Triangle: couch - kitchen - office. Many have been lost.

berpa: beach sherpa.

bion: the elementary particle responsible for short resumes.

bitee: one who is angrily bitten by a bitter biter.

bleachers: people who follow 45's COVID advice.

blent: the correct past tense of blend. "The milkshake was thoroughly blent."

bluffoon: a bluffing foon.

blunderbus: 45's campaign vehicle.

boavine: having the characteristics of both snake and cow; also long scarves that engulf you the way kudzu strangles a tree.

bonified: to turn something into a bone.

boom-meringues: pastries that fly off and return smacking you in the face.

boondocks: maritime terminus where boons are loaded and unloaded.

boor-ometer: scientific device that can precisely measure the extent to which someone is a total boor.

booster: ghost

boycot: cot where boy sleeps.

bozoas: microscopic idiots.

buffoon: a well sculpted foon.

caffiend: the dark side of coffee. (from cartoon by Hilary B. Price 4/18/21)

Calabash: to criticize California.

Calumny: more unfair criticism of California.

calypsofacto: "Of course we're going to dance."

campain: main reason why good people don't run for office.

canaryism: The belief that canaries will one day rule the world.

caninism: The belief that dogs hold the key to the solution of all the world's problems. "Go fetch clean energy, Rex!"

canonball: fundraising event celebrating church canons. (Look out for loose ones.)

cantelope (cant-elope): fruit used to discourage spontaneous marriages. "If you're worried about your daughter running off and marrying that idiot, buy some cantelope."

CAPITALISM: BELIEF IN THE POWER OF CAPITOL LETTERS TO MAKE YOUR POINT IN EMAILS AND ON TWITTER. Please stop. (See also capitalism: believed by the rich to be a perfect system for dividing wealth.)

cardinal number: whole number of cardinals at Vatican events.

carsick: car in need of repair.

casino: entertaining robbery.

cavitation: what happens to your teeth.

cello: "There's always room for cello." (Dale N.)

cerebellum: brain at war, see also antecerebellum.

cesium: chemical element responsible for arrests and seizures.

challahday: Jewish holiday.

challahpeños: spicy braided bread.

chicken coup: when chickens take over the government.

cleverish: having the superficial characteristics of being clever (sometime said about funny dictionaries).

ciudad: what you say when leaving your father.

chicken coup

clutterism: the belief that clutter actually contributes to quality of life.

codification: to turn someone or something into a cod.

codophile: lover of cod and codification.

collidoscope: police instrument used in the examination of collisions.

colonoscopy: the procedure used to remove all colons from a piece of writing. (See also semicolonoscopy.)

columny: defamation by a columnist.

complexify, complexification: to make something even more complicated than it needs to be.

condom-inium: where safe sex is practiced.

consciousness: the state of understanding what consciousness is without being able to explain it, thereby generating an industry of whacky pseudo-scientific and religious theories. See *The Origin of Consciousness: The Natural Selection of Choice Making Systems.*

consternationism: the tendency to take everything too seriously.

conviction: "Convicts sometimes go to jail for their convictions."

copulate: what police sergeants say when an officer is late for work.

corporeal: pertaining to a corporal. See also Private Parts, Corporal Punishment, Major Disaster and General Confusion.

cowrite: partial bovine authorship.

crastination: what those of us who delay are in favor of. "We are pro-crastination."

creche test: Can you name all the figures in a Nativity scene? What about Round John Virgin?

crewcuts: airline downsizing.

critical Mass: priest chastising congregation. (I thought of this cartoon before it appeared in *The New Yorker*.)

crop duster: person who cleans dust from crops.

crove: past tense of crave: "I crove ice cream all day."

culpable: responsible for culps.

cummmmmulative: correct spelling of cumulative.

cursery: where young children are taught to curse.

cyclop: the singular of cyclops. (See also Sighclop, famous world-weary horse.)

cycologist: one who counsels bike riders (from t-shirt).

darkism: belief in the power of darkness.

darkist: follower of darkism. (see also night person).

deadpan: frying pan that has been murdered.

debunk: to kick or drag someone out of a bunk bed. "The young boy had to be debunked in order to get him to school."

deadpan

decimating: the simultaneous wedding of 10 couples. (See also "hexadecimating," simultaneous wedding of 60 hexed couples.)

demoated: castle downgrade.

discombobulate: to undo any preceding combobulation.

distortionist: one who twists everything around for his or her personal benefit.

damask: fabric used for making masks; also in alternative anthropology Da-mask or "Father mask."

decalf: non-caffeinated young cow.

decrash: only permitted in states that have adopted the legal suspension of entropy.

defangled: the process of removing fangles, often for the purpose of replacing oldfangles with newfangles.

defeet: when your feet give up on you.

deprezzed: action removing a person from the presidency, as in a non-stolen election.

doggerel: poetry written by dogs.

dogma: mother dog.

doobedoobedoobedoo: wellspring of cool.

doomstrolling: strolling along, looking at your phone and not where you're going (into traffic, down manholes, off cliffs).

dosecent: person who can help you figure out the proper dosage for your depression medications.

doubloon: two bloons.

dreadmill: feared exercise equipment.

drivee: passenger who never stops telling the driver what to do. "Will you please shut up!"

dualers: people who fight over dichotomies.
'
dualism: belief system that everything in the world can be divided into two groups, e.g. those who believe everything can be divided into two groups and those who don't.

duelism: beliefs that provide a usually short-lived boost of confidence.

earring aid: device to assist in the putting on of earrings.

earnest: serious about earning money.

earphone: phone in the shape of an ear.

earplug: to promote ears on late night TV.

ebeing: electronic life form.

eggplant: factory where eggs are made.

elsewear: 3rd tier clothing where you
    don't care what you look like.
    "I'm just going to throw on some
    elsewear and go to the party. I don't
    care what they think."

emew: cross between a cat and large
    bird.

eggplant

emoots: emotional cow behavior.

emuting: expressing your feelings in a way no one can hear.
    "Click on unmute, you idiot."

enclapable: laudatory.

endful: opposite of endless. "He had an endful fascination with
    oil painting."

enigma: mysterious unfathomable mother.

enterplaining: complaining in an entertaining way. (Jerry Seinfeld 8/11/11 who went on to say "All comedy is enterplaining.")

envoyeur: peeping tom diplomat.

equalibrium: a drug that makes you feel equal to everyone else.

e-racist: a person who whitewashes current events and history to erase past and present racism.

errings: "I'm pretty sure I'm going to screw up tonight. I'm wearing errings."

eschew: express disapproval of food.

euphonium: substance responsible for fakes and frauds. "You phonium."

exami-nation: country where tests are always being taken. (See intestate).

factory: where actors are produced, (See also actory: where actors perform.)

falsifly: to submit fraudulent air travel reimbursement claims.

farcical: any popsicle that is used to satirize other popsicles.

faviary: place where favors are granted, often to birds.

fearies: disgruntled fairies who have become little scary flying things.

fewn: a small group of people, "the fewn."

flakery: any attempt to hide the fact that a person is a total flake.

flee speech. hateful speech that is quickly covered up by changing identities.

flooroscope: medical instrument used in the examination of floors.

figger: to calculate.

finditry: the art of finding things.

finitry: the art of the finite.

firebrand: trademarked fire. "If you burn yourself on a firebrand you may owe royalties."

flautist: "The flutist flouted being called a flautist. It's flutist, damn it."

fleeon: the most elusive of all subatomic particles.

Floridation: What happens to New Yorkers when they decide it's time to retire. "When my grandmother reached the age of 65 she was Floridated."

flutterby: what a butterfly does.

flutterism: flutterist: A person who goes from one thing to another, alighting only briefly on any one thing, and creating an air of nervous insignificance.

Font of all knowledge: from doctoral thesis formatting guidelines.

food court: where food is routinely tried and sentenced.

foxicity: poisonous news and opinions.

freeon: the most liberated of all subatomic particles.

frillism: belief in the supremacy of the peripheral.

funista: the gangland boss of fun.

furlong: needs haircut.

galore: abundance of dubious stories.

gerontosophy: philosophy of or about old people. Foundational literature on this subject was written by Publius Scipius in 120 B.C. when he penned "Questus Vetus Sugit" (Getting old sucks).

gesticulatte: to make wild gestures while holding hot coffee.

golf club: you can hit a golf club, join a golf club and get a golf club club soda.

goonery: (1) nursery for young goons. (2) firing range used by 2nd Amendment goons, where the "well-regulated militia" wording is conveniently ignored.

goutage: a brief break from gout. "Oh, thank god."

green bean: inexperienced bean.

gremlin and kremlin: can't be an accident.

gritz: NYC grits.

gyratical: the characteristic of spinning wildly about. (the first word I made up a million years ago.)

hasbins: storage area for the washed up.

hair traffic controller: maître de at barber shop.

hopeless: (without hope) and hapless (without hap).

haberdasher: one who runs like a haber, also member of the city of the Haber football club.

hair traffic controller

habit: something one professes to want to change but never does.

hackneyed: to be kneed in the groin by a hacker.

haggard: one who guards the hag.

haiku: A poem that is....fun but often cryptic and....oh so pretentious.

hairport: place with hair arrivals and departures. Security protects against bangs; pilot crewcuts required.

hamster: a guy who loves ham.

hayste: to hurry while the sun shines.

headquarters: opposite of hindquarters. "No wonder they were losing. The whole operation was being run from hindquarters."

heiring: descendents with the intelligence of small fish.

heirloom: device used to create previously unknown descendents.

high dudgeon: prisoner chained to wall near ceiling.

high jinx: upper levels of jinx.

highlight: flashlight used when stoned.

highway robbery: to steal a highway and put it somewhere the cops will never find it. "Bwaahahaha."

hijack: how you greet Jack.

hippocampus: the grounds of Hippo University

hippodermic: large bore needle. "Get me the hell out of here."

hip-po-pot-e-mousse: large French chocolate dessert.

homeopathetic: effectiveness of alternative medicine against real disease.

homeostasis: the act of staying at home.

hippocracy: form of government ruled by hippos.

hornet. a dangerous flying brass instrument; tend to nest in concert halls.

howbowchoo: "How about you?" in American.

Humorocity: humor's capitol city.

humeroids: can develop from low-grade humor like you find here.

humidor: damp matador.

humongoose: very large goose.

iceberg lettuce: prohibited food on ships at sea.

ideasophy: the love of ideas (needed because the word "ideology" has already been rudely taken).

impailed: walking with one foot in a bucket.

imagination: an imaginary country.

impoochment: removal of a dog from office. (They can be such a distraction especially when they're also president.)

imposterines: imposter tangerines. (You know which ones I mean. They are sometimes insultingly called "cuties.")

inbetweenism. the condition of being caught hopelessly between two or more states with no way out. (rock and hard place) (see also "amphibianism.")

indesquishable: incapable of being squished (James Cordon Mar 2021) a shared characteristic of rocks and hard candy.

influent: a person who practices influence. (See also affluent and effluent.)

injest: to pretend to eat for fun.

inundate: to date a nun.

insame: the insanity that results from trying to be like others.

intestate: legal status of people who die from testing.

in-the-wayism: belief that it is OK for people to walk 2, 3 and even 4 abreast on sidewalks, in shopping malls and airports, mindlessly blocking the way. Extra points awarded for stopping to laugh at stupid jokes.

intimi-dating: dating above your pay grade.

inviolet: safe from ultraviolet radiation..... and certain flowers.

iodine: to dine on credit. "I owe, I owe, so off to work I go.")

irksommellier: annoying wine expert.

i-toaster: metaphor for electronification of now easy-to-use everyday devices. Make sure your toaster has a good internet connection. And don't forget your toaster password. (See also Password Apocalypse.)

irksommellier

jaded: wearing too much jewelry.

jailopy: run down prison.

jamboree: festival celebrating jam.

janitour: excursion visiting well known janitorial sites.

jargone: unintelligible language used by management consultants, also
missing glassware.

jestate: clown pregnancy, also what you say just
after dinner.

jitterbug: insect best known for its dance steps.

judgement: proper way to spell judgment.
Whose idea was it to get rid of the "e"?

jukebox: box where they keep jukes when they're
not being used. (See jokebox: where they keep comedians when they
are not joking.)

Karma Sutra: sex acts that will get you punished in the next lifetime.

kazoo: Gesundheit!

kelp: how whales call for help.

kindread: fear of family members.

King Kong: worst airplane food ever.

kneedy: emotional state of persons before and after knee surgery.

knickknacks: small useless souvenirs that your children will throw away after you die.

knowledge: the ledge you stand on when you know too much.

knockneed: masochist desire.

das Kapital: book in ALL CAPS.

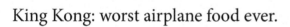

lactose intolerance: possible civil rights issue.

LISTEN --- SILENT: same letters. Cool!

lacerate: to cut someone with a frilly cloth.

lacrosse: game with sticks in which the players would much rather be hitting each other. See also hockey.

licori: plural of licorice.

life: a pre-existing condition.

limpidity: the state of limping.

literati: elite of those who litter, erudite litterers.

loaner: solitary bank official

low jinx: less-funny jinx.

L
I
S
T
E
N
T

S
I
L
E
N
T

macarune: pastry in the shape of a riddle.

mac and cheese: eating cheese while working on your mac.

malestrom: male created vortex of chaos and destruction. (See also "usual state of affairs.") (Conclusion: only women should be allowed to run for public office.)

Magnetism: a religious belief system focused on forces of attraction and repulsion. Adherents are known as magnetics.

mall-eable: easily manipulated into mall shopping.

masscara: makeup worn at church.

masticate: to slowly chew the central beam of a sailing ship.

Mathodist: religion devoted to mathematics, and $\Sigma\pi$ (some pie).

mayfly: seasonal insect responsible for airport delays.

Mathodist church

mayhem: agitated state of chaotic uncertainty about whether or not to add an edge to a piece of cloth.

mayhum: chaos or craziness caused by incessant humming.

meatloaf: meat not trying very hard.

meba: slang used when amoeba greet each other, "Hey, meba."

median strip: naked people in the middle of the road.

mementos: candy that helps you remember.

meon: elementary particle responsible for identity.

mermaid: services underwater hotel rooms.

metaphysical: the most thorough possible medical examination.

meteorology: the study of meteors. Who made this the study of weather?

metrognome: rhythmical gargoyle.

mewt: a speechless cat.

mewtant: genetically irregular cat.

mickey mouse: poisonous mouse.

microchasm: vast disagreement over the smallest things. (See Congress.)

microchip: what Bill Gates has on his shoulder.

midshipman: sailor who spends his entire career in the middle of the ship.

mimeograph: ancient means of copying, first developed by the Romans.

minimum: contest winner for the smoothest use of arches (mn) and poles (i).

minisculiscope: More than a magnifying glass but less than a microscope.

mishap: occurrence where you missed the hap by a very small amount.

misplace: where your keys and socks go to die.

misstrial: winner of annual legal beauty contest (obs.).

money market: place where you use money to buy money. Also place where you can squeeze money to see if it's ripe.

Monopoly: game where all but one player wants to scream and turn the board upside down. (See also "capitalism.")

moofter: organ in cow that makes the "moo" sound.

moo-on: elementary particle responsible for cows.

moron: elementary particle responsible for stupidity.

mortalize: to make something mortal.

motherland: where your mom comes from.

mountaineering: high and crazy at the same time.

mule deer: OK which is it?

multiverse: poem with more than one verse.

mumbo jumbo: very large mumbo.

mummy: well preserved mother.

mushroom: Iditarod rest area.

myassma: quagmire of disrespect for motherhood.

mystery: It's never the butler.

mystique: a mysterious antique. "I got this mystique at the yard sale and have no idea what it is."

nail polish: brightly colored paints used by carpenters.

napotism: letting your family members take naps before anyone else.

napster: expert napper.

night crawler: those leaving the bar at closing time.

nihilism: belief that there is no value in anything but yourself.

nightmare: scary horse.

nitrous oxide: high that makes you **think** you're not feeling any pain.

nonconductor: someone who is unable to conduct an orchestra.

nonexistence: the past and future of existence.

normalize: e.g. to make fascism seem normal in a democracy.

noshae (nosh-aye) (plural noun): things you can nosh.

novice: no-vice.

nai-eve: sometimes credulous belief in the Garden of Eden snake story.

namby-pamby: a pamby that exhibits the characteristics of namby behavior.

napkin: a relative you nap with during the day.

neighbor: the horse next door.

neology: study of the new. See also neologist and fashionista.

neosophy: philosophy of the new; an oxymoron since philosophy is obsessed with dead authors who have already thought of everything.

neuroasis: refuge for neurotics.

newfangled: having new fangles, see also defangled.

nickname: what you call Nick.

nomad: a person who is not mad.

neighbor

oaforism: aphorism about oafish lazyism.

obreys: a donkey's act of obedience.

oblication: travel that **could** be a vacation except for the fact that it involves family or other **obligations**, usually very expensive. (See also aggravacation.)

oscilatte: coffee of highly variable quality.

October: should be the 8th month of the year. WTF.

octopuss: cat with only eight lives.

oldfangled: opposite of newfangled, see also refangled and unfangled.

oh-zone: space where someone pauses to actually think (obs.).

oiligarchy: government ruled by oil companies (see USA).

olfactory: factory where smells are made.

omen: random signal preceding random event, imagined patterns of which reinforce supernatural beliefs.

omnibus: public conveyance.

oneteen: eleven.

opportoon: one who takes advantage of opportunities.

optick: plainly visible parasite.

orcarina: musical instrument played by whales.

organ recital: gathering of old people talking about their medical conditions.

oragnism: transpositional ectoplasm.

orson wells: underground sources of liquid orson.

otter space: where otters live.

ottoman: cross between a man and an otter.

outliar: someone who used to deny telling lies but now openly admits it.

Out of Bounds: autobiography of a retired kangaroo.

oxymoron: unvaccinated idiot who gets the virus and is surprised when he or she is put on a ventilator.

packrat: rat who will carry your possessions while you hike.

palindrone: flying object that goes forward and backward at exactly the same speed.

pandamonium: chordal harmonic instrument played by pandas at the time of their annual rampage.

paradox: two doctors.

panned pizza: pizza with unfavorable reviews.

pantaloon: song bird of the far north known for wearing trousers.

paradigms: 20 cents.

parasites: two sites.

parboil: golf term for rage at failing to make par.

parallelogram: means of communication between geometric shapes.

Pastafarian: follower of the Flying Spaghetti Monster.

passtor: out of date clergyman.

pastorize: to turn someone into a pastor.

Password Apocalypse: the coming domination, not of robots, but of technoroyalty who require incessant, unnecessary and maddening updates to all of your software and new passwords every time you sign in, that ultimately leads to the end of the world.

pedometer: device that counts children.

penchant: cheerleading chant at pen celebration events.

penmanship: special cruise for scribes and calligraphers.

penultimate: the second best writing implement ever.

peppermint: place where pepper is minted.

persnickety: according to snickety.

pheromoan: subtle chemical signal given off by chronic complainers.

Phodder: run of the mill academic output.

Phog: dissertation confusion.

picayune: your choice, any une.

pickle: you can eat a pickle and be in a pickle. "If you happen to be in the pickle you are eating, what happens next?"

pie: mathematical dessert.

pigment: statement about a pig.

pigpen: writing implement used by pigs.

piety: respect for pastry.

planetarium: glass enclosed case where planets are kept and fed three times a day.

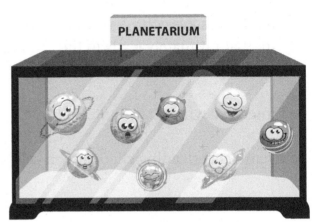

plaster of Paris: Do the people of Paris (my favorite city) know that their city is somehow known for its plaster. Sacré bleu!!!

platytude: platypus with attitude.

plakate: to soothe people by acting like Katherine Hepburn.

playpen: where they keep actors when they're not on stage.

Plutocracy: government ruled by Disney characters.

poetic justice: where prisoners are forced to read bad poetry.

pole vault: vault where poles are kept.

poltroon: the pole on which you hang your troons.

polygony: geometric shapes in multiple relationships.

pondage: enslavement in a pond. "The frogs were trapped in pondage."

pontification: to turn someone into a pope.

pontificrate: the box where the Pope keeps his crap.

pooter: a negative spoilsport type person.

poorous: characteristic of republicon social policy that allows people to slip through what there is of a safety net into poverty.

post apocalyptic: mail received after the Apocalypse.

postdoc: doctor at military posting.

post doctorate: diploma sent by mail.

posturized: theraputic treatment for slouching. "As he got older he slouched more and more until his wife finally got him posturized."

potash: what's left after smoking a joint.

preadolescence: before the hard times.

predation: the act of predating a document.

preeminent: not yet eminent.

preempt: just before your car runs out of gas, coming right before "empt."

pregnant pause: the first reaction of a male when hearing female spouse or partner is pregnant.

prefined: to be penalized in anticipation of an infraction.

prefix: to fix something before it is broken.

prisom: jail for light.

problematic: machine that automatically creates problems, often sold on late night TV as a "Prob-lo-matic."

prostate: gland that governs feelings of approval for government.

protest signs: End War - End Poverty - End Road Work (cartoon pending).

prunage: old age.

pshychology: psychology for shy people.

psillium: dietary supplement for clowns.

psionide: Greek poison.

psychosclerosis: hardening of the mind.

puntificate

pucillanimush: contemptible porridge.

puck: invisible object used when playing hockey.

pundemic: uncontrollable spread of contagious puns.

puntificate: to obnoxiously dominate the conversation with puns. (Who me?)

Quado: the fourth museum you visit in Madrid.

quadrant: to rave furiously about things divided by four.

quagmire: mire full of quags.

qualifly: to earn your wings as a pilot.

quandary: the clothes you washed that you're not sure what to do with.

quartet: French for 4 sided head.

quintessential: the fifth most essential thing.

raisin: a type of sin often associated with willful dehydration.

rambunkious: wild sleepover.

ramshackle: ankle monitor for goats.

randoom: arbitrary extreme bad luck.

ravenous: condition of predatory ravens.

reality: that which keeps getting in the way of our preferences.

recant: to put the wine back in the bottle.

rechoired: mandatory repeat choral performance.

ravenous

reckless: lacking reck.

reclusology: recluse science.

recycle: to bicycle the same course again.

red herring: the star of the show, standout performance.

redoubt: to doubt again.

refrogerator: appliance used to turn princes back into frogs. "After Prince Charming cheated on Snow White, he was placed in the refrogerator."

rehearse: to drive the hearse again, maybe going to the right cemetery this time, also practice for the next funeral performance.

relation-ship: vessel that can be used to carry away unwanted relatives.

relent: to lend again against your better judgement.

reinvinted: to rebottle wine.

repercussion: "Sorry, another one of your children just took up the drums."

repetititive: the way it should be spelled. (See acummmmulate above.)

repercussion

repoach: repeat offense against the King's deer.

republicons: party policy for those who are easily duped.

rethink: to set aside prejudices and think anew (obs.).

retired: to be tired again.

restraint: to strain again. "Apparently restraint is strainful."

retreat: to keep giving out Halloween candy to the same children who come back to your door over and over again, usually teenagers without costumes.

revamp: to vamp again.

rezoom: to continue the meeting but even closer up.

Rhodeside accident: scholar in a ditch.

rhubarb: noises made backstage to simulate the sound of an offstage crowd. Other vegetable names may be used subject to audition.

riding crop: next generation of up and coming horses.

ringleader: the person with the largest collection of rings.

roadents: bad drivers; also car damage.

robocalls: the worst fear of baseball umpires.

rubber match: almost impossible to light.

rubberneck: medical condition caused by looking at too many roadside accidents.

ruffage: high fiber for dogs.

Rumpelstiltskin: iconic fairy tale figure, also skin disease.

saddle: to deliberately make someone sad but in a teasing sort of way.

safeguard: bank security officer.

sagebrush: implement used to brush sage.

saloon: "At the end of a hard week of work, where do loons go?"

Santa cruise: a cruise ship filled with all Santas.

sarcoughagus: burial container for those who die of respiratory ailments.

satellite parking: area designated for parking satellites.

saucerization: (former surgical term) actually describes aliens boarding their space ships.

Santa cruise

scallywag: a movement of the tail indicating that a scally is happy.

scentry: guardian of smells.

screenie: will watch anything on screens, if properly provisioned.

semi-permanent: makes no sense since permanent is, well, permanent.

sez: purportedly representing uneducated speech. Sez who?

sighclone: an emotional storm of dissatisfaction and regret, also a sad twin.

shoperone: someone who accompanies you to the store and passes judgement on everything you buy..... and then tells your parents.

shurebird: self confident seagull.

silliquism: the stuff of word play, including unique silly sayings (as in this very book).

sink hole: where the water goes down at the bottom of a sink.

skulldrudgery: repetitive mindless activity, like accounting work or reporting for fox news.

skullduggery: to deeply inquire into another's thoughts or feelings.

slapdash: to escape after slapping someone.

sleeping bag. "Try not to wake it up."

slobster: untidy crustacean. (H. Richards)

snorage: the power of snoring (and snorers).

snowbank: open for snow deposits and withdrawals.

sobligations: obligations that make you weep.

snorage

sofari: a journey in which you have "so far" to go. "The family of 5 crammed themselves into a small car and started off on a sofari." "Are we there yet?"

somnambulance: ambulence specially designed to treat injuries caused by sleep walking.

sooee generis: uniquely piglike.

sould: completed transaction with the Devil.

speckulate: to make guesses about small things.

spellingbee: smartest of all bees.

spendthrift: sort of like freezinghot or wastekeep.

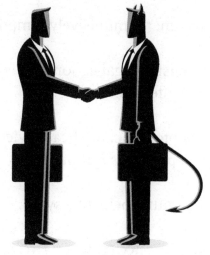

sould

spinal chord: the harmonic sound made by vertebrates.

spudology: the study of potatoes. (See also spudist.)

Statute of Limitations: law designed to keep really stupid people from taking office (later repealed).

steeple: to make something steeper.

stewpidity: lacking the mental acumen to cook and therefore not allowed in the kitchen.

straw breeze: actual phonetic pronunciation for strawberries. Also windy hay field.

strip mall: for undressed shoppers.

subdude: a cool person below the Dude. "The Big Lebowski was the Dude. I was just a subdude, heavily subdued."

substitoot: this year's replacement for New Year's Eve noisemaker.

swhim: to impulsively jump into the water.

swimsuit: legal action involving swimming offenses.

symptomatic: medical device that automatically produces symptoms.

symptum: belly of a symp.

swhim

synchroniceity: when two people are actually nice to each other at the same time.

syntax: money owed for correct sentence construction.

talibanism: It's OK to deny women's rights based on your own fanatical religious beliefs. (See also republicons.)

taxee: person who is taxed and may need a ride.

teabasco: weakest of all the hot sauces.

Terrapin: Earth Day lapel pin.

therewith: "Who went with you to the beach today, Tommy?" "I went therewith my mom."

thermocouple: lovers in a hot tub

thermocouple

thesaurus: most grammatically correct and nuanced of all dinosaurs.

thesaurus: dinosaur who also elevates your word usage and then eats you.

thoughtfull: state of brain when it's all filled up. Sorry, no more room.

thunderbolt: metal fastener used to hold lightning in place.

thunderclap: applause for thunder.

thymetable: a reference guide telling you when to use certain spices.

timekeeper: one who possesses[3] a cage for time, who feeds and grooms time and lets it out to run wild in the world from time to time.

toadstool. a bar stool where frogs sit and drink fine wine with their flies.

tofuel: soy based gas.

untoldings: stories that have never been told.

transcendental: When tooth pain gets so bad you actually leave this plane of existence.

trapezoid: device for trapping unsuspecting geometric shapes.

tollepathy: method of paying highway tolls with your mind.

topical storm: gathering of headline editors.

toreadoor: the doorway out for frightened bull fighters.

trickeration: an incidence of trickery. (Tom D.)

toreadoor

troopela: a small troop of Jewish boy scouts. (Thanks, Mom!)

truthiness: shallow ideas having the "feel" of truth. (Stephen Colbert)

turmoile: Not someone you would trust with your newborn son.

twitter: 280 characters or sounds made by small birds, whichever makes more sense?

---

[3] Notice that 5 of 9 letters in this word are s's.

udder: to speak about cows.

undawnted: not discouraged by the start of a new day.

underageous: outrageously too young. "Her attempt to buy beer at the age of 10 was underageous."

unherd: when a large group of animals remain silent.

unigoat: can be passed off as a unicorn with small children.

unintelligible: I love this word for reasons that are impossible to explain.

unitailed: having only one tail.

unitarian: having only one tarian.

universe: poem with just one verse, also where we live.

unwreak: to attempt repair on a large scale.

upgrade: K-11 graduation.

uptick: higher order insect.

usefull: If something is useful it should be given full credit with two l's.

usetabees: people who once were something else (name of NJ bar).

vacation: a trip where you pretend not to think about work.

vacuum packed: packed with nothing.

vacuous: mindlessness removable with vacuum cleaner.

vaguegrant: someone who is chronically unclear; also funding for unspecified purposes.

vamoose: to run away from wildlife, esp. in the north.

vandalize: to make someone into a vandal

vangourd: the lead gourd in a line of advancing gourds.

varmint: place where they produce freshly made vars.

varsity: team of upper class vars.

verbiage: a type of garbage. "Honey, did you take out the verbiage tonight?"

vertigo, vertigoing, vertigone: the three stages of falling down.

vignette: short theatrical performance involving salad dressing.

vindication: vacation where you had something to prove. "I finally jumped off the high diving board and climbed Mt. Everest."

virust: microbe responsible for iron deficiency.

waistfull: fat.

waterpipe: pipe used to smoke water.

whateveritis: annoying fatalism.

whippersnapper: a young and inexperienced person considered to be good at snapping whips. whispersnapper: a young gossip. whimpersnapper: a young whiner.

windsock: a sock the wind puts on its feet so it can put on sneakers and make a quick getaway.

waist: the part of the body where excess food goes to die; see also "waistland."

walnut: wall enthusiast.

wanton: ingredient of Chinese soup eaten with abandon.

water bed: where water sleeps at night.

water closet: where water is kept on hangers.

waterproof: mathematical demonstration that something is wet.

watertight: drunk on plain water.

websties: mucked up websites.

well done: a compliment - a steak order - and a dried up well.

well rounded: condition caused by overeating.

weti: yeti of the sea

wheeler dealer: tire salesman.

wheelwell: As the underground supply continues to sink, airlines are forced to dig deeper than ever for wheels.

whethervain: implement used to test humility.

whoopsea: to fall into the ocean.

wimper: one who wimps. "See you later, Mom. I'm going out with a wimper."

wincery: medical office.

wistful: full of wist.

woofer: dog.

world: The introduction of the letter "l" into the middle of the word "word" creates a linguistic micro-truism that the world is what is spoken. (Linguistic time travel to an ancient mindset or just total B.S.)

worryism: the belief that constant worry will protect you from the things you worry about. (See also alarmism.) Both normal states of being.

wreckoning: the consequences of destruction.

xenothon: a race to experience as many foreign cultures as possible. Also a multicultural fund raising event.

xerography: the sayings of the Greek playwright, Xerox.

Xorcize: obsessive exertion at the gym intended to cast out self-doubt and other demons.

XRay: to remove Ray, image-inative punster, from party invitation list.

xylophone: next generation of cell phones. No need to download ringtones.

xerox
xerox
xerox
xerox
xerox
xerox
xerox
xerox
xerox
xerox

yabba: a form of dabba doo.

yak: Asian mammal that won't shut up.

yester: old person.

Yesterday: annual holiday to commemorate yesters.

yikes: more than one yike; see also unyikable.

Yosemite: a member of the Yosemites, believed to be the lost tribe of Israel.

you-all: y'all. the doubled plural of you in undeserved disrepute. (I use this all the time.)

youthanized: to be made youthful.

zealot: a person who is willing to kill you for being disagreeable; see also "teenager"

zinc: place to wash dishes.

zooloft: animal anti-depressant, also second story in lions' cages.

zoology: the study of zoos; correct spelling "zooology" now in disuse. Current spelling also references collection of related books as in "trilogy." The exact value of the number "zool" has been lost, but it was more than three.

zygoat: domesticated, horned single cell animal.

PART II

Weird Word Associations
and Aglomerationisms
(Make up your own jokes.)

abject........object

academic....... anemic

airline........hairline

angle..... angel

area..... arena

antidote....... anecdote

augh..... laugh

auntie...... anti

Aye.....Oui (I.....we)

B B B B B B B

ballet..... bullet (Bullets over Baryshnikov}

banana..... bandana

beau..... rainbeau.....beau-tie

beget...... baguette

belief..........belie......lie

borders........ boarders

bobble....... babble

Bonaparte....... blown-apart
(Those in the company of Bonaparte were often blown-apart.)

bread..... dread

brie..... brief..... briefs

can knot....... can not knot

canary......... cannery

catchup..... ketchup

chased .... chaste

cello...... jello

chicken........ check-in

chilly......chile (Chile is not chilly.)

collision ..... collusion
(The crooks colluded to collide and
produced a collusion collision.)

comic........cosmic

comma........coma

complaint........ compliant

concussion..... percussion.

confers...... conifers
"Will you please get this tree out of our conference room."

confinement..... consignment

continent......... incontinent

conviction ..... convection...... confection

coral........carol

cow........ calcium........ cow-see-um

crow..... crowed....... crowd

curse...... course

daft..... draft

decision..... derision

defend..... defund

delirious .....deleterious

depot........ despot
(Please leave your despot at the despot depot.)

devil........ evil

diet....... die

disparate........ desperate

drive...... derive

earlier....... oilier

engage........enrage

exist........ exits

expense.... expanse

fertile...... turtle

few..... feud......fuchsia

fixed....... foxed...... outfoxed..... outfixed

father..... farther

flea------------------> flee

focus...... ficus

gallon........ galleon

gell.........jealous

gluten........ glutton

gusty..........gutsy

happiness..... haplessness

hello´........ hell´ low (Are you there?)

heroin....... heroine

host..... ghost

immoral...... immortal

important...... impotent

incompetent..... incontinent (e.g. South America)

inequity........ iniquity........ inequity....... iniquity (repeat)

infection..... inflection

infernal......... eternal

ingredients...........gradients

inveterate.........invertebrate

iron........irony

ironic....... iconic

issue........ tissue

juggler.......jugular
(When attacked by a gang of clowns go for the juggler.)

kibitz..... kibbutz

kidnap....... catnap

knowhow..... no way, no how

laudatory...... lavatory

law..... lawn

lawn order..... law n' order

loose....... losing ....lost

leopard........ leotard

litter...... liter...... lighter

lucider...... lucifer

manger..... manager

marina........ marinara

mealtime..... meantime

meddlesome...... mettlesome

meditation....... medication.
(One is what you need if the other doesn't work.)

milestone........ millstone

mobster....... lobster

monastery........ monetary

monk..... monkey

mother...... smother

mystification........ justification

namby........ pamby

nameless.........aimless......... shameless

noodles....... oodles

nun........ none

oral........ aural

orthodox......... paradox

outlaw......... outgnaw

oxtail..... loxtail

paced........ paste

pawns........ prawns

paws...... pause

peasant........ pleasant........ pheasant

perfect........... prefect

perspicacious........ perspiracious

polo........ polio

porch.... pooch..... smooch

preparations........ reparations

preposition...... pre-position

principal......... principle

prison..... prisom

quint..... squint.
(Look closely and you can see there are five of us.)

quirk..... quark
(Quarks are quirky.)

rabbi ...... rabbit

reckless.......... wreckless

refer...... reefer

rescue....... recuse

residential ..... presidential

saint........ stain

SANTA ..... SATAN !!

seeded rye........ ceded wry

should...... shoulder

sure........ shore

silver..... sliver

solder.......... soldier

sorted........ sordid

spacious..... specious

strange....... strangle

sting........ trusting.

surgeon.... sturgeon
(e.g. Sturgeon General)

tax..... taxi

taxes..... texas

temper..... tempter

throne........ thrown

tofu...... snafu (soy mixup)

TEACH..... CHEAT (yikes!)

topical....... tropical..... typical

torcher....... torture

touch...... ouch

trail...... trial

travel........... travail

uphold..... holdup

vetch..... kvetch

nexus....... vexus

vignette...... vinaigrette

VIOLINS...... VIOLENCE (from Baltimore Art Museum)

wonton...... wanton....... wanton soup

warming..... warning (as in global)

waste..... chaste.......chased

weeding....... wedding
(Insert your own joke here.)

wince....... once

witness ....witless

word..... sword
(Don't bring a word to a sword fight.)

word......... world

yaw.... yawn

zero........ hero

zoom..... doom (Ross F.)

AGLOMERATIONISMS

aviation.....bifurcation.....citation.....dissertation......fabrication.....
generation......hesitation......incarnation..... incarceration.......
jesticulation........meditation..... obfuscation......penetration....
sanitation......tabulation.......validation

bead.....cede......deed.....feed.....greed.....heed......lead.....mead....need.....
peed.....seed.....teed.....weed

bill..... dill...... fill...... hill...... kill...... mill...... nil......pill.... sill.... till......will

boom.....doom......loom.....room....tomb.......varoom.....womb......zoom.....
kaboom

ego...... egoing...... egone........ he gone

hired......fired.....mired.....sired..... wired..... tired (life?)

conception..... deception.........reflection

mastication.........domestication.......fantastication..........prognostication........
pseudosophistication

smoosh........ smooch........ shmoo...... shampoo

strongmen...... henchmen...... boatsmen......doormen......
plainclothesmen...... boogeymen...... linesman...... highwaymen......
journeymen...... omen...... and rejected-of-men (Handel) (Why are
there no wo-men?)

More UP words: Act up..... Add up..... Back up..... Beef up..... Bone up.....
Bottle up..... Bottoms up.....Box up.....Break up.....Brush up..... Bubble
up..... Buck up..... Bulk up..... Bundle up..... Burn up..... Carve up.....
Catch up..... Chain up..... Charge up..... Change up..... Check up.....
Cheer up..... Chew up..... Chop up..... Churn up.....Clam up..... Close

up..... Conjure up..... Cook up..... Cough up..... Cover up..... Crack up..... Cramp up..... Crumble up.....Curl up..... Cut up..... Dig up.....Dish up..... Divide up..... Divvy up.....Dredge up..... Drink up.....Dust up..... Eat up.....Fatten up..... Fed up.....Fess up..... Fill up..... Finish up..... Fire up..... Flair up.....Fog up..... Foul up.....Free up.....Freeze up..... Freshen up..... Fry up..... Fuel up..... Gang up..... Gas up..... Gather up..... Gear up..... Grind up..... Grow up..... Gum up..... Hands up..... Head up..... Heads up..... Heat up..... Hiccup..... Hole up..... Hook up..... Hurry up..... Jack up..... Jam up..... Jazz up..... Join up..... Jump up..... Keep up..... Ketchup..... Lace up..... Lap up..... Lather up..... Leg up.....Lick up..... Light up..... Lighten up..... Liven up..... Load up..... Make up..... Mark up..... Match up..... Mess up.....Mock up..... Mop up..... Move up..... Next up..... Offer up..... One up..... Open up..... Pack up..... Pass up..... Perk up.....Pile up..... Pin up..... Plug up..... Pony up..... Pop up..... Prop up..... Pull up..... Pump up..... Put up..... Rile up..... Rest up..... Rev up..... Roll up..... Round up..... Run up..... Saddle up..... Save up..... Scare up..... Scarf up..... Scoop up..... Scrape up.....Screw up..... Seal up..... Serve up..... Set up..... Sew up..... Shape up..... Shoot up..... Shore up..... Show up..... Shut up.....Sit up..... Slice up..... Slip up..... Smash up..... Sober up..... Spice up..... Split up..... Stand up..... Start up..... Steam up..... Stink up..... Stock up..... Straighten up..... Suck up..... Suit up..... Sum up..... Tack up..... Talk up..... Team up..... Tee up.....Throw up..... Tie up..... Time's up..... Touch up..... Tune up..... Turn up..... Up beat..... Up chuck..... Up end..... Up scale..... Up sell..... Up side..... Up stage..... Up start..... Up State..... Up tick..... Up turn..... Uppity..... Up yours.....Walk up...... Warm up.....Wash up..... What's up..... Wipe up..... Wise up..... Write up..... 7 UP (180) (Thanks Tom D.)

PART III

Funny-sounding Actual Words and Frazes.

(Just read this list out loud)
(Some of these words also appear in sections I and II.)
(This can also be read as one long poem,
with suggested breaks marked with a dashed line.)
(You can also rearrange the order of the words in any way you like.)

asinine

bobble

boogaloo

brouhaha

====

conniption

cockamamie

collywobble

comeuppance

crustacean

====

discombobulated

doohickey

====

feckless

festooned

flabbergasted

flummoxed

fiddle faddle

fuddy duddy

gobbledygook

====

herky jerky

hodgepodge

hoity toity

hoodwinked

hooey

====

hornswaggle

hanky panky

higgledy piggledy

holymoly

hullabaloo

====

kazoo

kerfuffle

knickknack

kumquat

loopy

mollycoddle

mumbo jumbo

namby pamby

nincompoop

peccadillo

====

persnickety

phantasmagorical

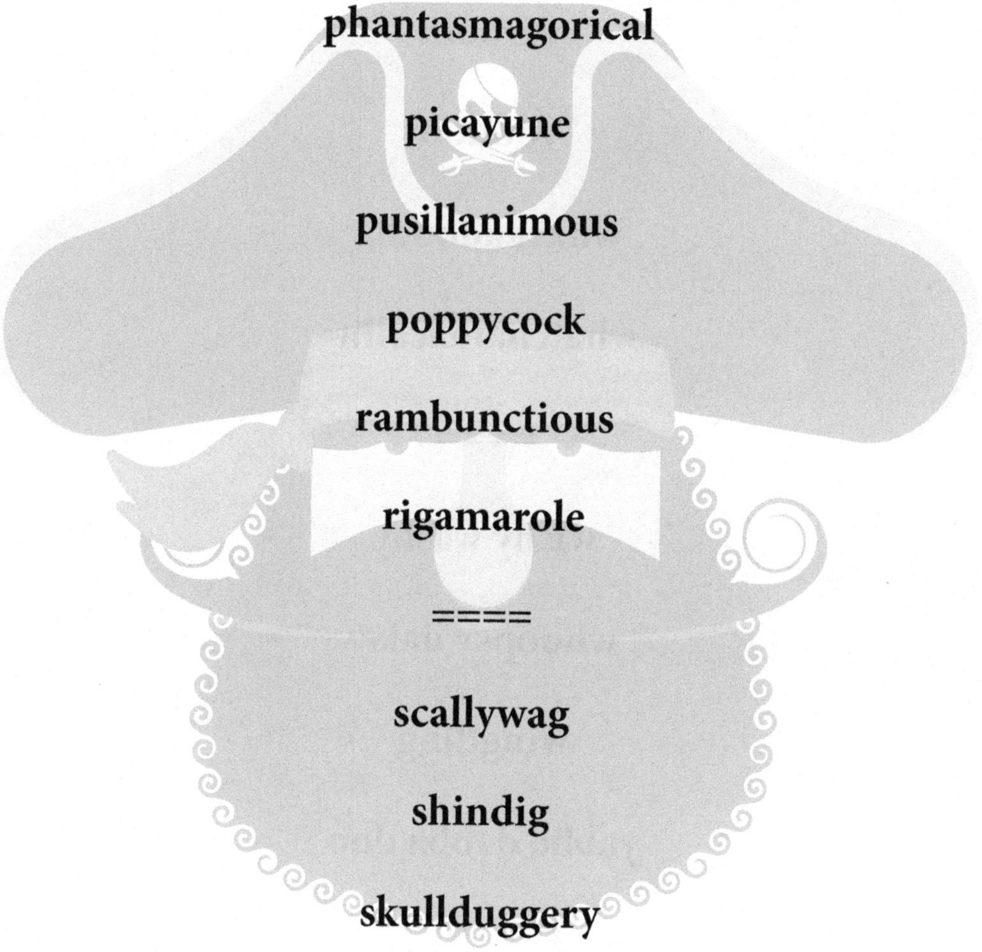

picayune

pusillanimous

poppycock

rambunctious

rigamarole

====

scallywag

shindig

skullduggery

smithereens

squiggly

super duper

thingamabob

====

vamoose

varoom

voodoo

whackadoodle

whatchamacallit

====

wishy washy

whoopsy daisy

wingding

yabba dabba doo

PART IV

APPENDIAGES

What if things had business cards?

Time: Turning things that could happen into things that did happen. Serving customers since "the beginning of time." Open every day except Christmas.

> **Time**
>
> Turning things that could happen into things that did happen.
>
> Serving customers since "the beginning of time." Open every day except Christmas.

Earth: The planet you live on. We provide places for you to do things. Services available above and below water. Contact Dph. Chrreeee-reek and Sons for more information.

Water: Bringing hydrogen and oxygen together for billions of years. Drink us or float on us. We don't care.

Fire: Hotter than you think. Lifetime services available: cooking to cremation.

Butter: Spreading joy for generations. Available in yellow.

Pork: The other white meat. So what! We're not chicken.

Chicken: At least we're not fat.

Air: You can't get by without us. Now 25% pollution free.

Wind: In your face, muthafucca! Service available from all directions.

Sun: Free light and energy for everyone. Beat that. Lifetime warranty.

Kindness: Being nice to kittens since 1634. Will consider other life forms on application.

Dirt: We've never seen a mess we didn't like. If you're tired of clean, call us. Service reps on hand in 49 of 50 states.

Clocks: We know where you live. If you're late, it's your own damn fault. New models available with nanosecond hands for greater precision.

Clocks

We know where you live. If you're late, it's your own damn fault. New models available with nanosecond hands for greater precision.

Cold: Freezing your ass off and loving it. Great for making balls and cubes.

Colds and Flu: We're sick of you when you're sick of us. Making life miserable since before you were born.

Never: Stopped in its tracks. Not gonna happen. Not never. Don't hold your breath. Too bad. Get over it. Stop whining. In 12 exciting colors.

Lists: Because you need us, we've got attitude. We'll get you organized. We'll keep reminding you. We'll make you pay for your laziness, you miserable excuse for a human being. Now, get started before it's too late. (Notice: Substitution for pianist allowed in some states.)

Dictionary: a reference book containing words usu. alphabetically arranged along with information about their forms, pronunciation, functions, etymologies, meanings and syntactical and idiomatic uses. We take "being correct" to a whole new level.

Encyclopedia: We know things you don't. *Nya. Nya.* Try writing a term paper without us. (Sorry, never heard of the internet.) Bursting with subject matter that can barely be contained on the page. *OMG! They've escaped! We can't have all that knowledge on the loose! There will be mayhem.* We have multiple personalities. We know we need help.

Bad Medicine

Forgivamycin: When used under the supervision of a priest clears the patient of all sins

Pryagra: Enhances patient's ability to know things about his or her neighbors.

Kleptomycin: Reduces the urge to steal other people's property.

Jingomycin: Transforms one's love of country in to a hollow shell of blatant self interest.

Malapropalox: Reduces the inappropriate use of large words.

Carnivoractone: Treatment for veganism.

Hippomycin: Kills bacteria responsible for weight gain.

Rectocrainalox: Treatment for "head-up-ass" disease. (Prescribed at 43's and 45's Whitehouses to little effect.)

Bagelox: All purpose Jewish medicine.

Megawhinealox: Kills bacteria responsible for incessant whining.

Tryagra: Enhances ability to try harder even if it produces no results. Consult a doctor immediately if trying harder lasts more than 4 hours.

Pyrocillin: Kills the bacteria responsible for people spontaneously bursting into flames.

Cryptomycin: prescribed for people who say things that make absolutely no sense whatsoever (also used at 43's and 45's Whitehouses).

Calibrex: Allows you to do simple math in your head. The cost of a bottle of 24 capsules is $39.95. If Johnny's train is going 75 miles per hour and Billy's train is going 65 miles per hour, how long will it take the space capsule carrying the Burkoon civilization to cross the vernal equinox?

Tryopenen. can only be opened with heavy machinery and/or weaponry. (SNL)

The Washington Post's Mensa Invitational

Note: The following entries appeared in anonymous form on Facebook on 12/11/15 with no mention of copyright restrictions. I support the Washington Post as an online subscriber. I think it's important to support quality journalism in this age of endless lies from the likes of Fox. But if anyone at the WP finds my inclusion of these contest results objectionable, I will be glad to remove them. Contact me by email. I wonder if it is still possible to give credit to the people who submitted the words. More WP funny words can be found by searching for "Washington Post Funny Words."

A. **New Words:** The Washington Post's Mensa Invitational invited readers to take any word from the dictionary, alter it by adding, subtracting, or changing one letter, and supply a new definition. Here are the winners:

1. **Cashtration** (n.): The act of buying a house, which renders the subject financially impotent for an indefinite period of time.

2. **Ignoranus** : A person who's both stupid and an asshole.

3. **Intaxicaton** : Euphoria at getting a tax refund, which lasts until you realize it was your money to start with.

4. **Reintarnation** : Coming back to life as a hillbilly.

5. **Bozon**e (n.): The substance surrounding stupid people that stops bright ideas from penetrating. The bozone layer, unfortunately, shows little sign of breaking down in the near future.

6. **Giraffiti** : Vandalism spray-painted very, very high

7. **Sarchasm** : The gulf between the author of sarcastic wit and the person who doesn't get it.

8. **Inoculatte** : To take coffee intravenously when you are running late.

9. **Osteopornosis** : A degenerate disease. (This one got extra credit.)

10. **Karmageddon** : It's like, when everybody is sending off all these really bad vibes, right? And then, like, the Earth explodes and it's like, a serious bummer.

11. **Decafalon** (n.): The grueling event of getting through the day consuming only things that are good for you.

12. **Glibido** : All talk and no action.

13. **Dopeler Effect**: The tendency of stupid ideas to seem smarter when they come at you rapidly.

14. **Arachnoleptic Fit** (n.): The frantic dance performed just after you've accidentally walked through a spider web.

15. **Beelzebug** (n.): Satan in the form of a mosquito, that gets into your bedroom at three in the morning and cannot be cast out.

16. **Caterpallor** (n.): The color you turn after finding half a worm in the fruit you're eating.

B. <u>**New meaning for common words**</u>. The Washington Post also published winning submissions to its yearly contest, in which readers are asked to supply alternate meanings for common words. And the winners are:

1. **Coffee**, n. The person upon whom one coughs.

2. **Flabbergasted**, adj. Appalled by discovering how much weight one has gained.

3. **Abdicate**, v. To give up all hope of ever having a flat stomach.

4. **Esplanade**, v. To attempt an explanation while drunk.

5. **Willy-nilly**, adj. Impotent.

6. **Negligent**, adj.. Absentmindedly answering the door when wearing only a nightgown.

7. **Lymph**, v. To walk with a lisp.

8. **Gargoyle**, n. Olive-flavored mouthwash.

9. **Flatulence**, n. Emergency vehicle that picks up someone who has been run over by a steamroller.

10. **Testicle,** n. A humorous question on an exam.

11. **Rectitude**, n. The formal, dignified bearing adopted by proctologists.

12. **Pokemon**, n. A Rastafarian proctologist.

13. **Oyster**, n. A person who sprinkles his conversation with Yiddishisms.

14. **Frisbeetarianism**, n. The belief that, after death, the soul flies up onto the roof and gets stuck there.

EPILOGUE

...to be continued

Hope you had fun............. Has your life changed? Well, probably not. But you may have found a few favorites, and you should share these with your friends. Every little bit of humor helps these days.

Suggestions are welcome.

Thanks again!

Mark

Credits

Many thanks to all the people in my life who have put up with my puns and other verbal shenanigans over many years, and helped me finish this book, including Terry Wilson, Janet Friedman, Ken Friedman, William Friedman, Serene Friedman, Tom DiRuggiero and too many more to name. Thanks y'all.

And special thanks to Ross Feldner for his brilliant artistic composition of the book and cover, and for his amazing patience with yet another quirky author.

Other writing by Mark Friedman

*The Origin of Consciousness: The Natural Selection
of Choice-Making Systems*

Waiting for Waiting for Godot (1 act play)

That Play About Atheism (3 act play)

That Voice in Your Head (screen play)

The Miracle of Flight: Humorous meditations of a frequent flier

*Trying Hard Is Not Good Enough: How to produce
measurable improvement for customers and communities*

Turning Curves: An Accountability Companion Reader

More writing, music and art at markspage.org

Other books referenced in the text

Confessions of a Failed Saint, Terry Wilson

The God Delusion, Richard Dawkins

The Language Instinct, Steven Pinker
(All new parents should read this book and learn to
marvel at how their child learns language.)

Word by Word, Kory Stamper

Oxford English Dictionary by.... no idea